Zoom In on
Native American Leaders

Pocahontas

Jennifer Strand

abdopublishing.com

Published by Abdo Zoom™, PO Box 398166, Minneapolis, Minnesota 55439. Copyright © 2018 by Abdo Consulting Group, Inc. International copyrights reserved in all countries. No part of this book may be reproduced in any form without written permission from the publisher. Abdo Zoom™ is a trademark and logo of Abdo Consulting Group, Inc.

Printed in the United States of America, North Mankato, Minnesota
052017
092017

Cover Photo: Three Lions/Hulton Royals Collection/Getty Images
Interior Photos: Three Lions/Hulton Royals Collection/Getty Images, 1; North Wind Picture Archives, 4, 12; George Spohni/Anton Hohenstein/Library of Congress, 5; ODI/Alamy, 6; John Smith/Vitrual Jamestown, 7; Joseph Sohm/Shutterstock Images, 8; iStockphoto, 9; Library of Congress, 10, 14–15; Henry Schile/Library of Congress, 11; John Gadsby Chapman/Detroit Publishing Co/Library of Congress, 13; Richard Rummels/Library of Congress, 16; Robert Ford/iStockphoto, 17; Alek Seykh/iStockphoto, 18; Richard Norris Brooke/Library of Congress, 19

Editor: Emily Temple
Series Designer: Madeline Berger
Art Direction: Dorothy Toth

Publisher's Cataloging-in-Publication Data
Names: Strand, Jennifer, author.
Title: Pocahontas / by Jennifer Strand.
Description: Minneapolis, MN : Abdo Zoom, 2018. | Series: Native American
    leaders | Includes bibliographical references and index.
Identifiers: LCCN 2017931231 | ISBN 9781532120244 (lib. bdg.) |
    ISBN 9781614797357 (ebook) | 9781614797913 (Read-to-me ebook)
Subjects: LCSH: Pocahontas, d. -1617--Juvenile literature. | Powhatan Indians--
    Biography--Juvenile literature. | Powhatan women--Juvenile literature.
Classification: DDC 975.5/01/092 [B]--dc23
LC record available at http://lccn.loc.gov/2017931231

Table of Contents

Introduction. 4

Early Life. 6

Leader. 10

History Maker 12

Legacy. 16

Quick Stats. 20

Key Dates 21

Glossary 22

Booklinks 23

Index 24

Pocahontas was a
Native American peacemaker.

She lived in North America before the United States was a country. She is remembered for helping her tribe and the settlers get along.

Pocahontas was born
around 1596.

Her father was named Powhatan. He was the chief of about 28 tribes.

Pocahontas lived near Jamestown colony. It was in Virginia.

English settlers made
the colony in 1607.

The settlers needed food. So they **traded** with Pocahontas's tribe.

These groups often fought. But stories say Pocahontas saved a colony leader from being killed.

History Maker

Pocahontas got along with the settlers. But they later captured her.

They taught her English customs. Pocahontas also became a Christian like the settlers.

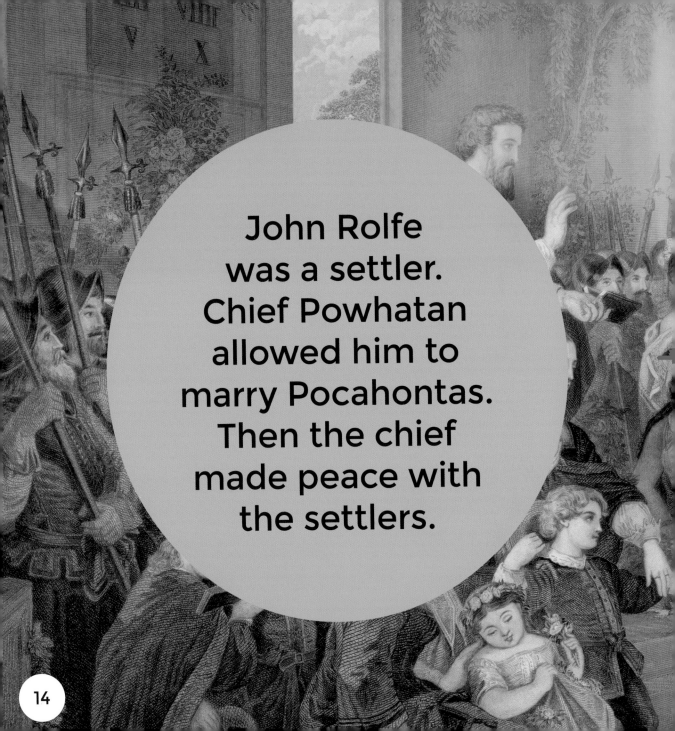

John Rolfe
was a settler.
Chief Powhatan
allowed him to
marry Pocahontas.
Then the chief
made peace with
the settlers.